FREE TO BE
CREATING A
BULLY-FREE WORLD

vicki abadesco!

Soul Shoppe
111 Fairmount Avenue, Suite 503
Oakland, CA 94611
www.soulshoppe.com
support@soulshoppe.com
510.338.3231

This book is published by Soul Shoppe
Copyright © 2012 Soul Shoppe

ISBN: 0-9710622-9-3

Cover and book design:
Ashley Inzer, www.thelaunchdesigner.com

CONTENTS

ACKNOWLEDGEMENTS

To all the wonderful people who generously contributed their stories to make this book possible, I say "THANK YOU!" Thanks for sharing your experiences and know that your story will touch hearts and save lives.

It definitely takes a village to raise a book! I am humbled by the community of people who supported me in this process - thanks to those who offered assistance, volunteered for tasks, took things off my plate and listened when I needed it. A special thanks to an incredible crew of people who had my back by staying up late, working through weekends, editing and editing again all while pushing and encouraging me along the way. Melanie Hopson, Heath Wood, Elizabeth Hubbard, this book would not have happened without you. I am so grateful.

To the Soul Shoppe crew, thanks for giving me time away from the mother ship so I could make this book happen. Special props go to Joseph Savage. Thanks for always being a pillar of strength and leadership.

To my family whose support I can depend on, thanks for always loving me.

Finally to Zoë and Asha and every child young and old, this book is for you. May you grow into a world that is kinder and gentler, more peaceful, loving and fun and one where everyone is truly free to be.

FOREWARD

I am honored and grateful to have been asked to write a
brief foreword to this important and inspiring book, Free
to Be: Creating a Bully-Free World. You have made a wise
choice in picking up this book--it will touch, move, and
empower you in so many ways.

Sadly, teasing and bullying cause a great deal of fear, pain,
and sadness for young people throughout our culture. As
a skinny white kid who played sports and attended inner-
city schools in Oakland, California, I took my fair share of
verbal abuse from some of the other kids on the playground
and in school. And while it rarely got physical and I es-
caped mostly "unharmed" in my youth, it made a lasting
impression on me emotionally and psychologically. In
those days--the late 1970s and early 1980s--there wasn't a
lot of awareness about bullying, and even fewer resources
and tools for how to address it. Thankfully, times are
changing, in large part due to the powerful and important
work of people like Vicki Abadesco!

I've known Vicki for over ten years and am awed and
inspired by her commitment to supporting, empowering,
and loving young people, parents, and school communities.
Her passion and creativity are remarkable and I've had the
honor of experiencing her work first-hand on many occa-
sions. The principles she teaches are universal, profound,
and easy to access. I wish Vicki had been around when I
was young and that Soul Shoppe could have come to work
with our school.

In my career as a speaker, trainer, and coach, I work with lots of groups of people, primarily in the corporate world, teaching principles of teamwork, communication, and trust. Some of the biggest challenges I find working with my clients stem from childhood trauma and fears of being judged, rejected, and hurt by those around them. As we address the issue of bullying with young people, we not only help release the pain of it in the moment, but also in the future. Free to Be: Creating a Bully-Free World is an important book for both young people and adults. It is filled with touching stories and practical advice. This book should be required reading for teachers, parents, school administrators, and young people alike. Thanks to the work of Vicki Abadesco and books like Free to Be, we truly can create a bully-free world!

Mike Robbins

Author of *Be Yourself, Everyone Else is Already Taken*

February, 2012
San Rafael, CA

INTRODUCTION

"You're so stupid. You are the stupidest person I ever met."

For a big part of my life, those words stopped me from taking risks, they held me back when I wanted to soar and kept me far away from pursuing big, bold dreams. Most importantly, they kept me from believing in me. No matter how much I had accomplished or how successful I might have appeared to some, on the inside I usually felt like a stupid little girl.

Growing up in my family, our basic needs were met: a bed to sleep in, food on the table, clothes to wear and two parents who were always there. My father made sure our family was cared for and provided much of the stability in our home. My mother played a different role. She suffered from several "nervous breakdowns" and was addicted to valium and alcohol. That was a prescription for unpredictable and psychotic behavior. I never knew when she was going to go off. She threw knives and other potentially harmful household appliances. She swung an axe around when angry and she made countless threats of suicide. I lived every day with stress, anxiety and fear.

As the youngest in my family, I was charged with being the caretaker of my parents, especially my mother. Every time she would pass out, I was there to soothe her. Every time she would have problems breathing, I would call 911. I'm sure other people were around, but I don't really remember them. I definitely felt alone and for a little kid, that was a big responsibility.

During my elementary years, I was more concerned about my mother's needs rather than my own. I would go to school without brushing my hair or bothering to make sure my clothes were coordinated and the other kids would notice and laugh and make fun of me.

In 4th grade I started to learn to make friends, mostly with kids from the neighborhood where I went to school. We would play high jump rope at recess and after school we went to each other's homes to play. It was fun to be accepted and to have friends.

Then one day I was kicked out of the group. I got the cold shoulder, the silent treatment and the looks that conveyed "you don't exist." I was heartbroken. My friends had become my escape from the heavy responsibility of caring for my mom on a regular basis. Without them, I was left to spend more time at home.

My exile didn't last long, but long enough to make me cautious of big groups of "friends." We never talked about what happened. I just remember there was another girl who was now on the outs. Apparently there was a revolving door of exclusion and these "friends" took turns pushing people through it.

I was always a compassionate person with a tender heart. As much as my mother put me through, I always sympathized and empathized with her pain. In high school, friends could depend on me to be a listening ear and a shoulder to lean on. It is in my nature to be loving and caring. As the peacemaker in my family at a young age, it's no wonder that I would grow up to start an organization that was built on compassion, socio-emotional learning and communication skills.

Everything I have gone through gave me skills to listen, to help, to encourage and uplift. All of my wounds are my gifts. Instead of being a victim to my circumstances, I choose to use my experiences to help and inspire others.

Every day at Soul Shoppe we have the opportunity to reach and teach the hearts and minds of elementary students. Through our character building and bullying prevention workshops and assemblies and peacemaker program, we reach 75,000 kids a year.

Every day we hear students courageously share their stories of what is happening in their lives. They ask for the name-calling to end, they share the reasons they come to school and bully, they ask to be treated with respect. They want things to be different and they need help.

Through the years, we have heard countless stories from kids. And, when speaking to adults, almost every single one can remember a time they were teased, harassed or bullied and the impact it still has on their lives today. Bullying has a long and lasting effect.

I wrote this book to not only show the impact that bullying has, but to emphasize what is really needed to end bullying--environments that nurture and foster the whole child.

There are no new skills, tools or techniques in this book, just the reminder that what our youth really need is time and attention from healthy, caring adults who are willing to listen. That's it. If we take care of our kids in this way, test scores would soar and bullying would dwindle. I guarantee it.

Each story you read ends with a lesson and a challenge. The stories can be read by young people, shared in a classroom or read at home. Some of the lessons are geared towards young people and most are geared towards adults. The challenges are meant for everyone.

My hope is that these stories will provide hope and inspiration. Any one of these stories could be your story. Truly, these stories belong to us all. Thanks for joining me. Here's to creating a safe, fun and bully-free world!

vicki abadesco!

FREE TO BE
CREATING A
BULLY-FREE WORLD

vicki abadesco!

CHAPTER 1
ROBERT

I'm alter-abled. I just started calling myself that not too long ago, and I like it. I used to say I was crippled. Other people would call me disabled or handicapped. I don't really consider myself to be disabled because I can get around just like everyone else.

I had polio when I was three months old, which meant my right leg basically stopped growing. My left leg is longer than my right leg, which makes me walk with a limp. At school some of the kids teased me and called me "handicap"--they didn't even know my name. Another

group of boys liked to call me "Little Robbie Shortstep."
They would call me that name to my face and run away
because they knew I couldn't run after them. I would be
furious. They liked to see me get red-faced and mad.

Still, I was no victim. In fact I was an angry, hateful little
boy, and no one was going to keep me down! At night
I would pray for my leg to heal or grow, and when that
didn't happen I was disappointed. I knew about anger
from my grandmother, who was raising my two sisters and
me. Her violence and abuse taught me to be an angry kid.
When I couldn't run after those boys who teased me, I was
determined to get back at them in some way. I would sit
behind one of them in class and when he least expected,
I would wrap my arm around his neck and choke him. I
would leave tacks on their seats, trip them in the hallway,
or let the air out of their bike tires. I had my ways of getting back.

Life was not fair. How could I live in a crazy home and be
crippled? Couldn't I just have one without the other? I
knew why I had one leg shorter than the other, although
no one really talked to me about it. Even when I went to
the doctor, my grandmother did all the talking. At home,
we weren't allowed to talk about it at all. When one of my
sisters tried to bring it up, my grandmother beat her. That
taught us all a lesson--just shut up.

Of course, it made sense that I didn't know how to talk
about being alter-abled to anyone at school, and no one was
going to talk to me about it, either. It seemed easier for the
kids to make sense of it by joking about it or making fun of

me. No one ever asked why I walked differently or what was wrong with my leg. I know people get freaked out when someone is differently abled and think it's rude to ask questions, but I would rather someone ask me about it than gawk and whisper in front of me because to me, that's being rude.

I always prided myself on being normal. I did physical labor for many years and kept up with the biggest and strongest guys who worked beside me. I earned the rank of 3rd degree black belt in three different forms of martial arts. I was in tournaments and won trophies. I was a skilled martial artist.

Through the years I have had to work on my hate and anger. My grandmother passed her bullying ways onto me, and my first wife suffered firsthand from that. Instead of using threats and intimidation, I had to learn to be a gentle human to others and to myself. I realized that it wasn't just my legs that were crippled, my whole mindset was. As I said, I'm no longer crippled, I am alter-abled. I appreciate my unique abilities, give thanks for my life, and count my blessings every day.

THE BALLOON

Robert had a lot of cards stacked against him. Studies show that students with both visible and invisible disabilities are at greater risk for being bullied. Students with any type of disability, such as multiple sclerosis, spinal bifida, cerebral palsy or muscular dystrophy just to name a few, suffer even more, socially speaking, than those that are not disabled. Students who are differently abled are often rejected or isolated by their peers and are bullied both verbally and emotionally.

We know that any type of bullying has a serious impact that can result in depression, loneliness, anxiety, low self-esteem, headaches, stomachaches, school absenteeism and thoughts of suicide. That's a lot for any student to bear.

Robert's disability began as an infant, and at a very early age he learned to adapt. He never really thought of himself as being different from the other kids until they reminded him that he was! No one at home talked about his disability, and it wasn't talked about at school either. He was left alone to try and deal with an incredibly burdensome pain. He felt anger, frustration and confusion, and he could have used a real friend to help him along the way.

Soul Shoppe teaches children about "The Balloon," a place inside where we hide the feelings and memories that we do not know what to do with. Like a balloon filling up with air, the more feelings we stuff down, the bigger our emotional balloon can get. When our balloon is full we have two choices: to empty it or to leak it. Emptying our balloon is a healthy way to release those hard emotions we are feeling. We can play sports, dance, scream into a pillow, or talk to someone. You know you are emptying because you are letting your feelings out and it doesn't hurt anyone, including you. Leaking is when you let out your unexpressed feelings in hurtful or harmful ways such as yelling, name-calling, gossiping and even physical violence.

Robert had a lot of unexpressed feelings in his balloon: his anger at being crippled, the abuse in his home, the teasing at school and his fierce drive to be like everyone else. Robert held on to all of those feelings, and along the way he leaked onto the people around him, including being abusive to his first wife. If Robert could have had the chance to truly express his years of grief, sadness and anger in a way that didn't hurt himself or anyone else, he might not have passed on the violence.

If we empty our balloons on a regular basis and feel heard and cared for, we can make better choices when faced with challenging situations. We can resolve problems in a positive way instead of by hurting, harming or bullying.

Our kids live with situations similar to Robert's every day. They carry so much on their shoulders. One way we can support them is by creating a regular check-in time in class or at home. By taking the time to do this, students can empty their balloon in a healthy, safe way. When that happens, there's more energy to focus on other things, like schoolwork or pursuing a dream or goal.

CHALLENGE

Think about what is in your balloon. Do you know if you have expressed anything that is in your balloon in a way that hurt someone, including you? What is something that will help you empty your balloon in a positive, healthy way? Maybe running, singing, listening to music, punching a pillow or having a good cry would help? Choose one thing you will do. Empty your balloon and *feel better*.

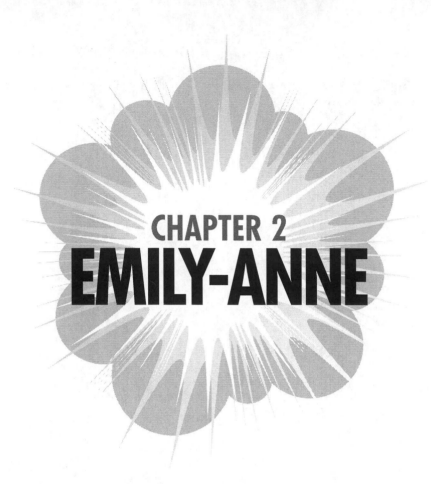

CHAPTER 2
EMILY-ANNE

W hat is wrong with me? What am I doing to make people hate me so much?

I could see the way they looked at me. I knew they were talking about me behind my back, but I had no idea what they were saying or why they were saying it. I did know that it had to do with how I looked. It was about my body--my weight. It was because I was "fat." They taught me "fat" and they taught me to hate it and to hate myself. I didn't even know that it was wrong to look a certain way. All I was interested in was laughing and playing with my friends, no matter what they looked like on the outside.

Because of my body, I was excluded from activities and I felt left out. Whatever self-esteem I had as a little girl began to crumble. I lived in dread that we would have to find a partner for a class project because no one ever wanted to be mine. How is a nine-year-old supposed to deal with that? I could hear kids say things like "Hey, why are you helping her?" The few friends that I had started to dwindle away. I was no longer Emily-Anne, I was a 'her' that people shouldn't hang out with or even be nice to. One after another, they shunned me. I blamed myself every day. As they treated me with such disdain and hate, I couldn't help but join in and hate myself too.

The good news for me in all of this is that my parents were great. Thankfully, I was able to talk to them about what was happening, and they stepped in. Even with their help and support, however, the situation didn't get better. The teasing continued, and the exclusion just got worse. I felt more alone than ever. The teachers couldn't make the other kids like me or be my friend. I remained on the outside. My parents saw how stressed and sad I was so instead of waiting to see if things were going to change for me, they decided to move me to another school.

That was really tough, but I'm glad it happened because things did start to change for me. I slowly started to make friends, and my self-confidence gradually increased. I was happy that I was making real friends who I could actually trust. These friends noticed I was afraid to speak up for myself and helped me to find my voice and my courage. They

helped me to believe in myself again. The more I accepted myself, the happier I became. At seventeen, I now
know the benefits of embracing who I am. Memories are
made to last--even the painful ones have a purpose. I've
learned to accept my body, and I even like having my
picture taken--that's a big step for me!

Because of what I have experienced, my heart goes out to
young people struggling with self-acceptance. I believe it
is my life's work to help others turn self-hatred into self-
love, so I founded WeStopHate.org, which is an online
grassroots movement dedicated to changing the way
over 100,000 teens view themselves. WeStopHate focuses
on self-esteem as a way to combat bullying because we
believe that teens who are happy with themselves won't
put others down.

When creating WeStopHate, I knew others could relate to
what I had gone through, so I chose to lead by example
by sharing my personal stories. I subjected myself to
ridicule by exposing my innermost thoughts and feelings
because I believe that honesty is the most effective way to
generate a sincere response. Instead of criticizing me, teen
viewers respected my authenticity. It was as if there was
a piece of me in each viewer.

I believe that WeStopHate is more than just an anti-bullying program. It's a call to action to stop hate--to stop
hating on yourself, to stop hating on others and to stop
letting others hate on you. Stopping hate isn't something
to do one time only; it's a practice and an approach to live
by each day.

In October of 2011, I was awarded the "TeenNick HALO (Helping and Leading Others) Award" for taking a stand for myself and other youth. I'm proud of all I have accomplished, and I'm happy to use my painful experiences to help others. If at any time you feel lost or confused, check out our site and see all the videos posted by other teens. You will see that you are not alone.

THE VISION

Weight is an obsession in our society. Our billboards and commercials are plastered with fast food chains encouraging us to super-size and taunting us with fried, greasy meals or sugary snacks. In another set of ads, we are bombarded with skinny actors and models that give us the message that we are supposed to look like that too. No wonder we have body issues!

In a recent national survey of overweight sixth graders, 24 percent of the boys and 30 percent of the girls experienced daily teasing, bullying or rejection because of their size. The number doubles for overweight high school students with 58 percent of boys and 63 percent of girls experiencing daily teasing, bullying or rejection because of their size.

We feel these negative messages about our bodies every day. We form part of our self-image by how others perceive, treat and label us. If people in our lives treat us poorly and view us negatively, we will most likely learn to view ourselves negatively. We learn self-hatred from internalizing criticism and abusive treatment from others. That's why it is so important to have a good friend in your life, and people who truly love and appreciate you just as you are.

Soul Shoppe begins nearly every program with what we call "The Vision." This is an affirmation of our worth, our potential and our real essence. It has five parts: You Are Smart, You Are Powerful, You Have What It Takes, You Are Important, and You Can Have A Fun & Happy Life. Imagine how different life would be for the entire world, if we all just had more of these messages in our lives!

Because she has taken a beautiful vision and shared it with the world, Soul Shoppe wants to give PROPS to Emily-Anne and her organization We Stop Hate. This young lady is a shining example of how powerful we all can be when we stop taking in the hateful messages that run rampant, and we start listening to the loving messages (like "The Vision") that fill us from the inside out.

CHALLENGE

Take a moment to list the ways in which each one of the statements in the vision is true about you. Which statements are difficult for you to believe? What kind of support do you need to see each of these clearly in yourself? Ask one person to support you to believe in that statement about yourself.

CHAPTER 3
AYESHA

My name is Ayesha and I'm ten years old. I'm just your everyday girl. My favorite colors are blue and red. My favorite animals are poodles and French terriers--they are so adorable! And my favorite meal is chick pea soup. Yum! As I said, I'm a typical girl who is usually happy and gets along with everyone.

One day when it was raining, I got on the school bus and sat down on a seat that was wet. I didn't know there was a leak in the roof of the bus that had soaked the seat with rain. As I sat in the puddle of water, my pants got wet.

Immediately a group of kids on the bus started laughing and teasing me, especially one kid. They called me "potty pants" and other rude names I can't mention here. I was embarrassed, hurt, and mostly really angry. When I got to school, my teacher could tell that I was very upset so I sat down and told her the story.

At lunch, I talked to my friends about what had happened. They listened and encouraged me to speak to the principal right away, so I did. After school that day, the principal got on the school bus and reminded everyone to show respect and to not bully or tease. I was glad an adult stood up for me and from that day on, didn't want that to ever happen to me or anyone else, so I decided to write a book about it called, "Buddy Bully." Learn more about it on my website www.ayeshareviews.com. Taking a stand for yourself is not always easy, but if I can do it, so can you!

THE POWER OF WORDS

Where is the line between teasing and bullying? Teasing can happen in ways that are playful and do not hurt anyone. Bullying, however, is never an enjoyable experience. If you look closely, you will see something associated with teasing that is not associated with bullying--friendship!

In this story, Ayesha was not describing an act of friendship. It was a random group of people who were not concerned with her feelings. They weren't empathizing with her at all, and she wasn't feeling safe. Friends would empathize. Friends care about how the other person feels. The motivation of these children was to laugh at and ridicule another person, and it was hurtful. The underlying motivation is the most clarifying distinction between teasing and bullying. Bullying leaves someone feeling embarrassed, angry, sad, upset and powerless.

Sometimes when we are hurting, we may use our words to hurt others. We use our words to put another person down, and for a moment, to lift ourselves into feeling superior. When faced with the reality of our actions, we try to cover it up by pretending we were just teasing. But the hurt feelings are proof that something else happened, something we call verbal bullying.

I wonder how many people would verbally bully people if they truly knew the injury they were creating. Ultimately, Ayesha teaches us all a sweet lesson. Rather than retaliating and continuing the problem, she used her words much more powerfully. She asked for help!

Letting another person know how you are feeling and what you need can be an immediate way to take hold of a painful situation. It can turn the tide rather than perpetuate a problem. It creates a doorway for a new possibility.

Her principal absolutely did the right thing. She used her words powerfully with a clean and clear motivation to make everything better and safe for all! Now, Ayesha will always have the memory of an adult showing her what care and respect are all about! Congratulations to Ayesha and her principal!

CHALLENGE

Can you think of an example where someone was being teased versus being bullied? Can you think of a person who often verbally bullies other people and laughingly calls it teasing? What are the differences you notice and feel when comparing these two situations?

Have you ever verbally bullied someone and passed it off as teasing? Today could be YOUR day to make it right. Make that apology!

Is someone currently verbally abusive to you? Today could be YOUR day to set the record straight. Ask for help in dealing with the situation, and let the person know how you truly feel and what you really need from them.

CHAPTER 4
JONATHAN

D id I even have a chance? Well, it sure didn't feel that way! Elementary school--ah, I remember it well. The isolation, the loneliness, the friendless-ness. When I was growing up, you could say that I was a walking bull's-eye for bullies. I was the low man on the totem pole--picked last for sports teams, pushed and shoved around, and called every name in the book. Most of the time I just checked out and disconnected. It would have been way too painful to take in their words and their harassment.

I was so clearly the kid that was picked on that, in the third grade, a rare "friend" kicked me in front of a group of kids so that they wouldn't think he was my friend. It was easier for him to kick me than to risk becoming the next target. To say that I lacked self-esteem would be an understatement. While my parents of course loved me, even my mother thought I was "slow" until I tested into the gifted program at my elementary school. Even though school was my personal hell, I still did well in my classes, and my only sense of self-worth through eighth grade came from being book-smart.

Things changed when I entered high school and somehow happened upon my school's small speech and debate team. I also discovered theater. Being involved gave me an outlet for self-expression and helped me to come out of my shell. While I was still teased by Tom, Chase, Andrew, Eric, and more (and by no means would have been declared popular), speech and drama gave me friends, a community, and a sense of self. I even went to the semifinals of the State Championships in speech a few times and found a girlfriend there and many friends from around the state. Things weren't so bad.

In college I majored in theater and competed on UC Berkeley's speech team. With focus and work, I eventually became one of the top collegiate speech competitors in California. I don't know what would have happened to me if I hadn't found speech and drama. It probably saved my life. Because of its impact on me, I became a speech coach for numerous schools, and my students have been both state and national champions. I eventually formed my own coaching business, and now spend my days helping people to find their voice and to speak from their power.

If you would have told me back then that I would grow up to speak in front of groups and to be in the spotlight, I never would have believed you! I was shy, introverted, and never wanted to be the center of attention. Being bullied shut me down and closed me up. Today I have a voice--and I use my voice to help uplift others. I'm able to give my students what I always wanted but didn't get: respect, a safe space and self-esteem. I'm proud that I can give my students the skills to speak their truth, and to help shy kids turn into formidable forces so they can shine in their own spotlight.

Where is your voice? Spend time with others who will listen to you. Do things that will help you find your own unique voice. Find something you love. Speech, basketball, dancing, computers, underwater scrabble--whatever it is, find it! Your voice has power. Once you find it, use it to help yourself and the world!

A DIAMOND IN THE MAKING

In a study conducted in home and schools, they found that on average, adults make only one positive comment for every 157 negative comments and commands to kids! Can you imagine? It's no wonder that many young people feel cynical, negative and hopeless. How many kids hide their true gifts and talents under their negative attitudes? How many are afraid to show their talents for fear of being rejected? How many gifts are overlooked and not really seen? Even Michael Jordan, one of the greatest basketball players of all time, was cut from his high school basketball team as a sophomore.

In this story, Jonathan was able to find something at which he was good. At the time he may not have known he was good at speech or debate, but over time and with some guidance, his natural talents flourished.

Truly seeing people and their talents is a powerful preventative strategy to bullying. Inside every person is a gift just waiting to burst forth, to be nourished and developed. Are you willing to look at others as a diamond in the making?

CHALLENGE

Do you have talents that go unnoticed? What does that feel like? Does anyone know you have these gifts? If you have a talent that you've been keeping under wraps, tell one person about it today! Is there someone you know whose gifts or talents go unnoticed? Make a point to reach out and let him/her know that you see his/her gifts and offer support to help them shine.

CHAPTER 5
ED

In elementary school, I was Mr. Popular. I got all the laughs. I had all the friends, and everyone loved and accepted me. I was funny, out-going, adorable, sweet and kind--the perfect little kid.

Then middle school happened. I was no longer Mr. Popular. In fact, I was Mr. Socially Awkward. I had to work hard to fit in, which became more difficult when other kids starting making fun of my name. It wasn't about my name, which is Ed. It was how they said it--in a whiny, annoying, high-pitched voice, "Eddddd." Was that how they looked at me? Was I someone to mock and make fun of?

I remember walking down the hall carrying my books when another male student looked right at me and said, *"Boys don't carry their books like that."* Wait. What? Huh? I had no idea what he was even talking about. I was just carrying my books.

Here I was in the 7th grade, feeling confused and trying hard to figure out what was going on. Kids kept making fun of my name. I could tell that they were talking about me, which made me shut up and shut down. The spunky popular me had turned into the quiet and shy me. Instead of jumping at the chance to be the focus of attention, I now laid low.

There was a cool 8th grader named Brent who was a star athlete, and he was nice to me. We ran track together, and although we weren't really friends, he would take a moment to encourage me or say something kind to me. He took me under his wing a bit, which was a big deal and meant a lot to me. I looked up to him and appreciated that he could be both popular and nice.

One day as I was in the school gym, I overheard a bunch of boys talking about the rope exercise in class. It went something like this:

Kid #1: How many could you do with that heavy jump rope?
Kid #2: I don't know, it's really heavy.
Kid #1: How many do you think *Edddd* can do?
Brent: That little fag probably couldn't even lift it!

Everyone: *Ha, ha, ha, ha, ha!*

They had no idea I was listening. I was mortified and totally bashed up on the inside. I couldn't believe they were talking about me like that and especially that Brent was. I looked up to him, and this is what he really thought of me? I really believed he was my friend and that he didn't buy into all this teasing and bullying. I was crushed, and I never spoke another word to him again-- not one word. Even when he stopped to talk to me, I just kept on walking and ignored him.

As I look back, I realize now that Brent was a good kid who made a stupid mistake. I don't know if he was try-ing to play a role or look cool with the other kids that day. Maybe he was just trying to fit in like the rest of us.

Thankfully, I survived the 7th grade. Summer came and went, and then something changed in 8th grade. It was as if 7th grade had never happened. The teasing stopped, people liked me, and I slowly started to regain my confi-dence. I still held back and never felt 100% comfortable to be myself. It wasn't until the 12th grade that I knew my personality was established and that people would just have to deal with me exactly as I am--funny, outgoing, adorable, sweet and kind.

FORGIVENESS

Sometimes we are right and sometimes we are wrong. We rise, we fall, we make mistakes, and we have opportunities to clean them up. As much as we feel we must be perfect, the truth is, not one of us is perfect. And yet, we live under this pressure on a regular basis.

In this story, Ed was struggling through 7th grade. His friend Brent brought Ed hope that there could be a way out of the lower social ranking he had at school. Brent had social status--people looked up to him. Brent's acceptance and friendship helped Ed survive that school year, right up until Brent said those seven words that crushed Ed's spirit. Brent made a mistake. When feeling pressured to do or say the right thing in front of our peers, we make mistakes, and quite possibly we hurt people in the process.

We don't know why Brent, with all his perceived social status, would choose to bash Ed rather than stick up for him. Maybe he didn't want to be left out. Maybe he didn't know how to stick up for Ed.

At Soul Shoppe, we teach children and adults how to use communication tools like the *I Message* and the *Clean Up*. The *I Message* helps us to stay connected to our true feelings and to ask for what we really need. Ed needed and wanted Brent's support. After that incident, Ed didn't have the words to communicate to Brent what he needed. As Ed looks back at that situation today, he knows that Brent was a good kid who did a dumb thing.

An *I Message* from Ed could have looked like this:
1. *I feel* angry
2. *When people* I consider a friend puts me down behind my back.

3. *I need* people to respect me and not talk about it.
4. *Please* respect me?

Brent's response would be the ***Clean Up***:
1. *I know that I* disrespected you by putting you down behind your back.
2. *I apologize.*
3. *What can I do to make it right?* At this point Ed would respond, "If you're my friend, then treat me as a friend and don't talk badly about me."
4. *Next time I will* be a friend, respect you and not talk badly about you.
5. *Will you forgive me?*
6. Ed responds with either yes or no.

What could have happened if Ed gave Brent an *I Message*? What could have happened if Brent did a *Clean Up* by admitting he made a mistake and asking for Ed's forgiveness? Can you see how they both could have benefited from that?

In our world, it seems there is little room for real forgiveness. In school, kids are made to cough up an insincere "I'm sorry," before they return to playing or hanging out. Adults threaten kids to tell the truth and then punish them when they do. There's no winning for telling the truth. There's no acknowledgement of how challenging it is to be honest and to call yourself out for doing something wrong or hurtful. There is no validation for the amount of courage it takes to ask for forgiveness. There's usually just shame and blame. No wonder no one ever wants to own up to mistakes.

We forget that forgiveness is healing for both sides. The person asking for forgiveness gets to right a wrong. They get to clean up the mess they made and recommit to the friendship with no more guilt or shame. The person who forgives gets their feelings heard. They get to ask for what they really need from the other person to make it right. Instead of being a victim, they are empowered. For both people, there is the possibility of a restored friendship and a new way of being with others. Over and over we have seen this very exchange of *I Message* and *Clean Up* bring friends closer, heal wounds, and stop horrible rumors, teasing and bullying.

Taking the risk to express ourselves has the potential to boost our self-esteem, renew friendships, put away old hurts and get us what we want and need.

CHALLENGE

Review the *I Message* and *Clean Up* and try it with someone in your life. Take a risk to ask for forgiveness or to ask someone for what you really need.

CHAPTER 6
MELANIE

Where did this kid come from? His name was Maki, and he was Japanese. He hardly ever spoke a word, but when he did he was difficult to understand. In our elementary school, there weren't any other kids who were like Maki.

I was a good kid, one of the top students in my class, and the first girl to get picked for every sports team. I didn't pay much attention to Maki--I mean, no one really did. He dressed like an old man in gray slacks and button down shirts, and he was kind of stocky and not good at sports.

He was in our class, we knew his name, but I didn't think about playing or hanging out with him--no one did.

What happens to a kid who gets left out and hangs out around the edges like that? I never knew what he did for lunch, and I don't recall him having any friends--I just remember that he was different, so I left him alone. Maki didn't talk a lot, but he was a smiley kind of kid, as if his smile was his only way to communicate with us. Because he rarely spoke, I made the assumption that he just wasn't smart. He didn't raise his hand, answer questions in class or have much to say during classroom discussions.

One day the bell rang for recess, and we all lined up ready to go out and play. When the teacher set us free, I ran barreling out onto the yard. Maki was already outside, just standing there minding his own business, but he was directly in front of me. I saw him. I knew he was there, but something in my mind registered that Maki didn't really matter, he didn't have much value, and he didn't deserve my respect. So in that instant, instead of running around him, which would have been easy for me to do, I ran right into him. Wham! It was full-on, body-on-body impact!

"MELANIE!!!" That was my teacher who saw the whole thing. I knew instantly in my heart and in my mind that I had done wrong. I was a good kid who did a stupid thing. I wonder how many other kids dismissed Maki like I did and felt it was okay to bully and disrespect him, even just one time.

Of course I apologized to him, and for the next few days

I felt horrible about what I did. Trying to make it up to him, when I saw Maki out on the playground I made it a point to say hi to him and smile.

Looking back, I can see clearly how Maki was an easy target. He was different from the rest of us. He didn't know the language very well, and no adults ever explained his situation to us. He wasn't dumb, like I assumed, he just didn't know English yet. It would have been fun helping him learn new English words, and he could have taught us Japanese! The cultural gap made him seem strange and odd. We knew he was from Japan, and there was probably an interesting story about how and why his family moved to America. But no one told us that story.

As an adult, I wonder what I could have learned if I had befriended Maki instead of bullying him. I regret the opportunities I missed in 5th grade to learn from Maki, to practice compassion, and to broaden my narrow world.

GETTING TO KNOW ME

Have you ever had another person make assumptions about you before they even got to know you? Have you ever had family or close friends make comments about you that made you feel like they don't really understand you? Putting labels on people is something we all do as human beings, whether it's total strangers meeting for the first time, or loved ones that have been around us our entire lives.

Research tells us that we form an assumption or judgment about someone within the first seven seconds. We may not have even spoken to them, and an assumption is already made! We all do this. It's just what our brain does--it likes to organize and put things into categories. The issue is what we do next with our assumptions and judgments. If we notice them and let them go, then we can be open to learn who that person is beyond what we initially perceive. We actually get to see them!

We hear kids labeled with names like "bully" or "trouble-maker" or "loser." When we do that, we never get a chance to see what is on the inside. In fact, we solidify that role and that identity for them. We think to ourselves that so-and-so is a real bully, and then we treat them that way. Often our labels encourage them to bully even more. If we are willing to attempt empathy and understanding, something amazing happens. We feel the assumptions drop, and the labels float away. We get to see, maybe for the very first time, who is actually in front of us. It is someone who has been misunderstand and judged.

Amazing and beautiful things can happen when we open our minds and hearts to others. We get to feel compassion. We get to share commonalities. We get to see that we are really more alike than we are different. We get to connect to a human instead of a label, and the separation between us disappears. Isn't that what we all want?

CHALLENGE

Notice if there is someone in your school or community that gets a lot of labels put on him or her. Notice the effect that label has had. What would it take for you to reach out to him or her and offer something that they usually don't receive? Maybe a smile or someone to just say hello. Take the challenge, drop your assumptions and labels and reach out to someone today.

CHAPTER 7
JEN

Who is that girl in the mirror? Does she really have a black eye, a busted lip and bruises around her neck? How did she get here? My name is Jen, and this is my story.

I have a mom, a dad, a step-mom, two brothers and a sister. I love my family and I know they love me. My parents did their very best in raising me. In fact my dad and step-mom pushed me to be the best and not to settle for less than perfection. I know those statements were meant to be motivating and encouraging, but most of the time all

I heard was that I wasn't good enough and that I sucked at every attempt I made to be perfect.

I did a lot to make my parents happy and proud. I went the extra mile. I practiced. I ran harder and played better. Mostly I was performing simply to get their attention. I was a kid, and I was desperate for the approval, care and love of my parents.

When I started school I was already on the "make everyone else happy" rollercoaster. I did things so that other kids would like me, even though they never really did. I was the brunt of their jokes. I wanted their approval so badly that when I was invited to parties, I always said yes hoping that it meant I was finally being accepted. At these parties I usually ended up alone and targeted for insults and humiliation. It sounds crazy, but whenever the next invitation came, I gladly accepted, hoping this one would be different.

By the time high school came around, I was willing to do anything to make people like and accept me. I really wanted to be "in" with the popular people. I pressured myself to look a certain way--to have the right haircut, the coolest clothes, and the perfect body. I developed an eating disorder and took pills to make me thin. The truth was that the pills didn't make me better--they made me sick. The other hard truth was that being thin didn't win me any friends. I didn't impress anyone, and the popular people weren't interested in being my friend. So I was left with my perfect jeans, perfect haircut and perfect body and was still being called names, laughed at, ridiculed, excluded and bullied.

Every day I would go home feeling alone and empty on the inside. And every day my parents told me to get over it and make new friends, which made me feel even more alone. In those moments I wish they had said, "Sorry it's so hard for you at school. We're sorry the other kids are mean and bullying you. We love you. How can we help you?" As a young woman trying to figure it all out and blaming myself every day, I longed for those words.

As I was desperately failing to win the approval of the popular girls at school, I started to turn my attention to the popular boys. They were willing to give me the attention I was looking for, and it felt good. That attention cost me some things, including my self-esteem and self-respect. How could I feel good when someone was treating me badly?

Years went by before I realized that I had allowed most of the guys in my life to insult me, bully me, disrespect me, humiliate me and mistreat me. This is what led to the scene of me staring at myself in the mirror bruised and bloodied. I was trying to get out of another abusive relationship when he told me he would kill me before he would let me go. After he had knocked me to the ground, kicked me and had his hands around my throat, I remember thinking that my life was meant to be more than this moment--I was meant to be more than this. As soon as I had that thought, he released his grip and let me go. The next day as I looked in that mirror, I swore that something like that was never going to happen again.

I started seeing a counselor who helped me heal some

wounds and also supported me to feel good about myself. Today, I'm still cautious of groups of people and afraid they might try to hurt or humiliate me in some way. Most of my life I never felt good enough to belong, and now, with the support of caring friends and family, I'm learning that the only approval I ever really need is my own.

HEART FELT

Our sister organization, *Challenge Day,* has a famous saying, a sentence that they encourage people to complete. "If you really knew me..." Take a moment and feel the depth of that statement. How do you feel about answering that question? Some people feel relieved by it because finally someone is asking! Others feel scared of the opportunity. It's understandable. We do not have much space in our lives to be open and honest about how we feel inside, yet sharing who we really are is essential to our well-being.

Jen's story is a perfect example of what happens when we place such strong emphasis on social status, what others think, or external authorities. We become more focused on what's "out there" than the value of what's "in here." We grow up not knowing our own heart. We have no idea what we really want out of our lives, or we are too afraid to admit it and go for it. Teaching a child to know themselves is one of the most powerful things that we can ever pass on to them.

Jen learned early on to accept criticism and to take harsh feedback. By the time she started going to school, she was already trained to deal with snickering comments and conditional relationships. She carried all of that into her adult life, which put her into dangerous and life-threatening relationships. Somehow, Jen learned that it was okay to be mistreated, put down and bullied.

What Jen wanted growing up, and what most kids want, is to be really seen and heard. Kids long for someone to stop, to put aside all distractions, to focus 100% full attention on them, and to hear their words, their needs and their desires. This action alone would decrease bullying. When you know yourself, when you are clear about what you really want, and when you surround yourself with people who support your happiness, you are less prone to bullying behavior and less likely to be a victim of bullying.

CHALLENGE

Commit to asking at least three people in your life this question, "If I really knew you, what would I know about you?" Give your full attention to them so they are able to respond authentically. Once they have answered, share your answer with them. Feel the connection you have made to each other. Families, make this a regular practice during meals or outings. Teachers, regularly incorporate this into your class. Friends, ask the people around you this question, and watch how much closer you'll feel to them and to yourself.

CHAPTER 8
CEDRIC

"**M**ud puppy! Freakin' mud puppy!"

What the heck is a mud puppy? I was in the 9th grade, and I asked my friend Kit to go find out why these guys were calling me a mud puppy. We'd already learned in biology class that a mud puppy is like a little salamander. Back in the day I was a scrawny kid, but I knew these boys were not calling me a salamander! Kit came back and told me it was their nickname for a "dumb-ass little nigger."

I grew up in the South and went to a mostly middle-class school. The student population was 70% white, 29% black, and 1% other. Though no one said it outright, it was im-

plied by some teachers and most students that the white kids
were smarter than everyone else.

Back to "mud puppy." This group of four white boys and
I were in algebra class together. I loved algebra and loved
being challenged to get the best score I could in this class.
After every exam, the teacher would write up the names of
the students who received the top points on the exam, and
I was proud that my name was almost always on the list. I
was proud to be doing my best. The four boys were never
on the list. That's when I started hearing "mud puppy," first
behind my back, then to my face. I would hear it in class, in
the hallways and any other time our paths crossed. At Hal-
loween I came dressed up as a giant. I had a costume that
extended my torso, and I was able to see out of the middle.
The boys looked at my costume and I heard them say, "Hey,
is that mud puppy? We should rip his arms off!" "Let's get
him!" Thankfully, they didn't touch me. At this point all
the bullying had been verbal, but after hearing that, I knew
something had to be done before it would escalate into
something else.

In my school district, at the beginning of every school year,
the students were given a student handbook. The handbook stated that every student has a right to attend school
in peace--free from intimidation and harassment. I took my
handbook and went to see my counselor, Mr. Britt. I told
him about the teasing and the bullying, and he asked what I
wanted to do. We decided to talk to the boys together to see
if we could put an end to it.

We had the meeting. I wanted to know why they were
harassing me. Their answer? I thought I was smarter than

them. Really? A person can't be smart without being harassed, taunted and bullied?

Mr. Britt backed me up all the way. He explained that if it didn't stop, the principal and their parents would be called in next, and the boys could be suspended.

I was proud I stood up for myself and had found a way to resolve this. I was also grateful to Mr. Britt for standing by my side. After that day the bullying ended, and I didn't have to hear the words "mud puppy" again. And I felt free to do as well as I wanted to in algebra class.

INHERITANCE

Did children invent bullying? We hear about these "bad" kids doing all this bullying in schools, as if kids themselves created bullying. Why don't we hear more about all the bullying that happens everyday in the adult world?

Nations threaten other nations. Races violate other races. Political parties are always at each other's throats. Everyone wants to be superior and better than everyone else. Is it any wonder that our children do the same thing when they come to school?

There are many things to pass along to our children and our future generations. We can pass on all the hatred, racism and bigotry that was passed on to us, or we can take all of the positive things that we have inherited and ensure that children receive these things.

This story is an example of just that! Somewhere along Cedric's path, he learned to use his brain to resolve problems. He used the intelligence that was passed on to him to do something clever that most of us would never have thought about.

Unfortunately, the other boys appear to have had a different experience. They had inherited something else--prejudice and racism. Even more deeply, they inherited *self-hatred*. I have never known a person who truly loved and valued their self to be jealous or envious of another, for any reason, let alone because they were smart! Quite the contrary! When people have regard for their own purpose and value, they instantly respect and even cherish others for their value. They willingly compliment and acknowledge others. It's just the way they are.

This is a great opportunity for us all to think about what we are passing along to our children, and what they are taking to school with them. Truly, bullying isn't something we are born with; it's something that we *learn* from watching other people. Let's give the world something better than all that ugliness. Let's leave this place even more beautiful than it was when we got here!

CHALLENGE

Consider all the character traits that were handed down to you. What are the ones you most appreciate and how do they show up in your life? From whom did you inherit that trait? Share with someone one trait you are most proud to have inherited.

CHAPTER 9
FLOR

Growing up in Mexico, life was not easy. Like most things, you just learn to adapt to your life. My mom worked a lot, and my dad would not win any awards for parenting. At school the kids didn't like me. They left me out of games and activities and pretty much ignored me. I mostly spent time by myself or with my sister.

I was glad to stay away from the other kids because school was hectic. Some kids would get into fights, some would talk about other people, and others would stir up conflicts or get in your face. As much as I wanted to belong, I didn't feel like I fit in. Teachers stayed away from the conflicts and rarely intervened. I never cared if the other kids talk-

ed about me to my face or behind my back. If they said a
single word about my sister - *that* would set me *off!* Hitting,
kicking, punching, slapping - I wouldn't stop until someone
pulled me off! I was a product of my violent environment.

You see, when someone has been hurt and the wounds are
both on the outside and the inside, it makes sense that they
would want to hurt other people in order to relieve some of
their own pain. Violence was the only way I knew to deal
with what I was feeling on the inside. If someone made me
angry, I didn't think twice about throwing punches or hurting them. It made sense at the time.

In my home I had to grow up fast. My mother eventually
left Mexico to move to the States for work. My sister and I
were left alone with our father. We were seven and eight,
and as I mentioned earlier, our father was not the best parent. We were basically on our own as little kids, and it was
a tough time. Even though I'm younger, I've always been
really protective of my older sister. Eventually my mother
heard how our father was treating us, and we came to live
with her here in America. It wasn't an easy transition for
me. I didn't speak English. I didn't know how to interact
with the other kids, and school was strange and new. I felt
different from the other kids, and when people sense you
are different, they stay away from you. That's what happened to me--the other kids just left me by myself. So, just
like with the kids in Mexico, I was ignored.

I adjusted, and through the years I eventually started making some friends. I'm a junior in high school now, and I
don't like to see the way people treat each other. Instead
of learning about someone who is from a different culture
or wears different clothes or does something different than
you, people find ways to make fun of them and put them
down. That just isn't right!

I've always stood up or spoken up for others who needed help. Now, I'm part of the Safe School Ambassador program at my school, and I'm trained to help in situations when someone is being put down or bullied in some way. If I don't help out, I have become part of the problem.

Where I come from and how I grew up, if somebody was beating you up, nobody else really cared. That's messed up. If I can help, I will help. What about you?

BRICKS & THE BABY'S HEART

When we are born, our hearts and minds are wide open. We are vulnerable, sensitive and open. That vulnerability is why it is so important to protect and care for babies. Unfortunately, more times than we would like to know, children of all ages are exposed to violence, yelling, arguments, abuse and much more. What does all of that do to a baby's heart?

As we grow older, and endure more and more pain, our heart begins to protect itself. It has many ways of doing this. It hides itself. It covers itself. It builds walls within walls within walls. Why? Because when it isn't safe, we start building a wall around our heart. At Soul Shoppe we call it *"Putting Bricks on the Heart."* Brick by brick, we build a wall to protect us from hurt and harm.

The wall may protect us, but it also creates and perpetuates a problem! The problem is that people stop caring, or rather, they forget just how much they do care. They start closing themselves off to other people, to opportunities, to themselves, to their own feelings and to their thought processes. We call it being "hard-hearted," but that's just another way of talking about having a wall built around our hearts, and a heart covered with bricks.

Every day in our programs we hear the heartbreak that our young people are living with--grief, violence, divorce, hunger, poverty, drug and alcohol abuse, racism, the list goes on and on. It would make sense that we would want to barricade ourselves from the world. It is tough out there! We must ask ourselves "is this what we really want? Do we really want to live a life of seclusion and exclusion? Do we really want to feel cut-off and isolated from ourselves and from others?" The answer, deep down, is a triumphant "NO!" and that is *exactly* what you will hear if you ask a group of children that question. They want love. They want to make a friend and to be treated with respect. That's it. It is that simple. The fortunate thing for us is that we have a way to make that happen.

Just as easily as bricks can go up, the bricks can also come down. If being hateful and cruel to each other causes us to put bricks up, then guess what causes us to take them down? Kindness. Caring. Support. Empathy. Love. Friendship. Help. Fun. Laughter. Have you ever had an experience where you were having a bad day, and someone, even a total stranger, did some small thing in a kind way, and it just made the *biggest* difference in your day? It is amazing how powerful genuine kindness is. It can melt your heart in an instant. The next thing you know, one by one, we begin to build trust again, and start *"taking down the bricks."*

Here are some helpful tips to take bricks down off of your heart, or the heart of another person who is near and dear to you:
1. Stop, drop and listen.
2. Take a moment, and ask someone how they are doing--how they are really doing.

3. Let people know how you feel, and what you need.
4. Ask specifically for what you need.
5. Apologize.
6. Ask for forgiveness.
7. Make it right.
8. Feel your feelings with an open and loving heart.
9. Help another person.
10. Do something you enjoy, with someone you love!

Most of us have learned to live with the bricks around our hearts and we forget they are even there. Take a moment and notice what bricks you no longer need and set yourself a little bit freer.

CHALLENGE

Take a look at this list and choose at least three actions you are going to do to take down some bricks. Let one person know what you are doing so he/she can support you to get it done.

CHAPTER 10
REBECCA

The Secret Club was created by the popular girls in 6th grade. Of course, all the other girls and I wanted to be invited into the club. And I was! Whew, what a relief!

Tracy lived down the street from me, and we were friends. The Secret Club wanted to vote on whether we should invite Tracy to join the club. Tracy was my friend, so I voted yes. The next day I got a call from the leader of the Secret Club letting me know that there was a vote on whether or not *I* should be in the Club. Wait a minute. What? Was I not supposed to be friends with Tracy? When do these kinds of rules get made?

The leader was sorry to tell me that I was voted out. She

told me that she voted for me, and it was the others who didn't want me in. I called every girl in that club, and they all said the same thing--each voted to keep me, but the other girls wanted me out. As I made each call, I became more scared, confused and humiliated. Why was this happening to me?

The next day, I showed up at school, and each person in the Club wouldn't talk to me, play with me or even make eye contact with me. It was as if they didn't know who I was. I didn't exist. When I approached the leader, she told me that the reason they couldn't play with me was because my socks didn't match. To this very day, I remember looking down at my feet and feeling embarrassed and blaming my socks for this terrible situation.

After that, school was never the same, and it never got better. Being an outcast was devastating. Every day I was filled with anxiety, and I felt sick to my stomach. I was always late for school because I hated going. I never felt safe in the cafeteria, and I can still remember what it felt like eating my lunch on the street curb because it was the only place I could go.

I made some friends throughout high school, but I no longer felt like I could trust people in the same way. When my friends in the Secret Club kicked me out and excluded me, something within me shut down. I made a point of graduating early from high school so I could get away from it all. In college I had a couple of friends, but I stayed away from all social events. I just couldn't do it.

I'm in my thirties now and have a beautiful child. I'm happy to say that I allowed my friends from college to become real friends. I'm still working on trusting people socially. I recently had a beautiful experience with a group of people that was healing and life-changing for me, mainly because I dropped my wall and let them in. I have a lot of compassion when I see others who also struggle with groups. I empathize with their anxiety and do what I can so they feel safe and included.

If I could do it all again, I would take my lunch, sit down with those girls, and tell them that they were being mean and cruel. I would tell them they had no right to treat me or anyone else in that way. I wish the adults in my life had done something. My mother listened and hugged me, but she never approached the school or the other parents. She confirmed my belief that nothing could be done and that I was powerless. I wish my teachers had noticed the girl on the curb eating lunch alone. I wish the teachers had noticed how the Secret Club was picking off students one by one. I wish somebody would have gathered us all up and talked with us about what was happening.

For any teacher or parent out there reading this, please notice. Please see us and don't ignore the sign of someone sitting alone.

IN / VISIBILITY

When I read this story, I can picture Rebecca as a sad and lonely girl sitting on the curb outside. A girl no one sees. A girl no one notices. How many of these students walk our halls and streets?

Feeling invisible is one of the strangest and perhaps most painful experiences anyone can have. Being ignored and excluded can simply crush a person's sense of worth. The first thing we do is blame ourselves. We ask, "What did I do wrong?" We imagine how we could have done things differently. "If only I had done this _____ more" or "if only I had been less ____" then everything would be okay. We can go on forever blaming and shaming ourselves, but the simple truth is it's not our fault.

Feeling alienated is one of the most significant predictors of academic failure. When young people feel like nobody cares about them, the natural consequence is that they feel they don't belong. How could a person succeed academically when they feel that way inside all day long? They can't!

There are many things we can do to be inclusive. First, it is important that we notice when someone is physically standing to the side, or usually without friends. Next, we can be willing to ask them to join us, ask them to play, or ask them how they are feeling and why they are sitting away from the group. Often, these kids on the periphery might pretend to be okay or refuse our efforts at first, but that's just their defensiveness from feeling hurt and unwanted.

It's important to continue to encourage excluded youth to join in and to continue to express to them how much they are missed and what a valuable part of the group they are. When they begin to see an actual contribution that they can give to the group, they will inherently value it. Let's take the time to find out what they do well and what they feel proud of, and then help them to see and remember it.

We can also help with other kids on the spot or perhaps behind the scenes to empathize with the excluded child. Sometimes there are past conflicts that have occurred, and the kids have not shared it with anyone. Empathize with the children who do not want to be with the excluded child and then assess the problem. For example, maybe the other kids say that the excluded child is always a sore loser, so they don't want to play with him. Knowing this information will lead to helping the young people solve the problem.

By taking time to notice the kids left out on the edges, you can change their entire experience of themselves, school, life and the world!

CHALLENGE

Have you ever been excluded or left out for any reason? Can you remember what that feels like? Do you ever feel like that in your life now? Surprisingly enough almost everyone feels left out or alone, even when surrounded by lots of people. Send a text to some friends and remind them that you are there to listen if they need you. Remind them that true friends are there to get each other through tough times. By starting this chain, you might help someone in need, including yourself.

CHAPTER 11
LANI

I lived in a normal neighborhood where the school bus picked kids up, and we played outside after school. The Smiths were our neighbors. They seemed normal enough from the outside. Mr. Smith was an airline pilot and ran the local karate studio and Mrs. Smith worked at home. At times, things with the Smiths got weird. Mr. Smith drank a lot, and sometimes we would hear screaming, fighting and things breaking in their house. They had three kids: James, Patrick and Ruby. We saw how things at home affected the three of them. Mr. Smith made sure all of his kids were trained in karate, and they were aggressive and sometimes violent. One day while playing outside, James got mad at his little brother Patrick and shot him in the eye with a BB gun!

Ruby and I would hang out and play together. We were friends. Sometimes if I wanted to play with other kids, she would get really mad and tell me that I couldn't have any other friends. I wasn't sure what to do when Ruby would say things like that because I didn't want her to get mad.

One thing Ruby and I had in common was that we both liked riding horses. Our parents signed us up for lessons and competitions. I really loved to compete. At one point I was the Pacific Coast Champion, and I was really proud of that! Ruby would watch me win, and I could tell that it made her furious, especially since she could never place. This became a problem because every time I would place or win, she would get in my face and tell me I was stuck up and that I better watch my back because she was going to teach me a lesson. I knew she was mad or jealous, but I never knew what to say to her.

The neighborhood could tell things weren't going well for the Smiths. I knew the whole family was having problems, and I would try to remember that fact when Ruby would threaten me or get in my face about something. At this point our family was used to their family and how they treated everyone on the block. Any time Ruby had something to say to me, it was usually a threat or a rude comment. It was best just to ignore what she said.

One day the school bus dropped us off, and Ruby and I walked towards our homes. She walked behind me, accusing me of thinking I was better than she was, and she told me that she was going to kick my a**. We were in high school now, and Ruby's threats were starting to scare me. Before I knew what was happening, Ruby jumped on my back, knocked me on the ground and started punching me in the neck. She used her karate training to hurt me. At one point she hit me so hard that I went unconscious.

Luckily, the postman saw what was happening, pulled Ruby off of me and called an ambulance.

Ruby had been harassing and bullying me for years. On that day she knew exactly what she was doing. At first the doctors thought I would have some type of paralysis, but I eventually got all the feeling back in my legs. I did lose my sense of balance and equilibrium. That may not seem like much, but it meant that I couldn't ride horses anymore or do anything else that took some sort of balance, like skiing or skateboarding. It took me five years to recover from that incident.

My dad moved us out of the house and far away from that neighborhood. We took the Smiths to court to pay for the medical bills and filed assault charges against Ruby. It was really hard, and I hated it. Our family didn't get much out of it financially, and the only punishment Ruby received was probation.

Being bullied and assaulted was traumatizing for my entire family, and we paid a high cost. I lost my horses, we lost our home, my parents had to get extra jobs, and I started working to help pay bills. Even though I know it wasn't my fault, I blamed myself every day for putting my family through this emotional and financial stress.

Bullying comes at a high price for everyone involved. Think twice before bullying. You may never know the impact it can have on someone. I wouldn't want what happened to me to happen to anyone else--ever.

THE PRICE OF BULLYING

Physical bullying has to be one of the most dangerous aspects in modern schools. Dan Olweus, perhaps the father of research and prevention on bullying in schools, estimates that in American schools alone there are nearly 2.1 million kids who actively bully other students, with 2.7 million children receiving the painful role of "victim." Other sources report that *1 in 20* students have seen another student with a gun at school. Even more staggering is that over 280,000 students are physically attacked each month in secondary schools. It is almost too much to think about.

To prevent bullying from ever starting, let's focus on the socio-emotional needs of our youth that are vital for their personal and academic success.

When children go to school, they focus on their academics because we encourage or force them to do so. This is not what comes first to them or what comes naturally to their minds. What is natural, and what does concern them the most is if they are physically and emotionally *safe*, if they have *friends*, and if people acknowledge and *appreciate* who they are beyond their academic achievement or any other sense of "earned" value.

Everyone loves and needs to have a safe place to go to. Everyone needs true friendship in their life. Everyone needs and enjoys being appreciated for who they are. When we lose these things, and these needs are not met, we become unhappy, sad, angry and lost. Most kids who bully others are young people who are going through painful and often severe difficulties at home, in their neighborhoods, and sometimes at school as well. This behavior can stop when we begin to ally with kids.

Imagine if Ruby had an ally. Imagine someone walking into Ruby's life, really assessing her situation, and getting to know her for who she is and what she wants in life. Then you would see what we at Soul Shoppe see every day--bullying behavior stops in an instant, and caring friendship begins as though it had never ended. You would see expressions of sorrow and regret for past behaviors. You would see forgiveness. You would see hope in the eyes of all involved. You would see what is possible for every child and school. Bullying is *not* who we are. Ever. It is something we do to try and get our emotional needs met when we can't find any other way to make it happen.

CHALLENGE

Go to someone you know and genuinely care for what needs support. Start a conversation with them. Tell them that you care. Listen. Tell them you want to help. Ask what they need to feel supported. Let them know how you want to support them. You might say something like, "You can always come to me if you need a friend to listen," or "If you just want to cut loose and have some fun and forget about it all for a while, I'm here." Everyone has a particular gift to offer as a friend. Find out what yours is, and give the gift.

CHAPTER 12
MICHELLE

It was 7th grade, and Hannah, Rachel and I were three peas in a pod, or so I thought. I began to suspect something was up when I would call one of them to suggest we all get together, but they were already hanging out. This happened a few times, but I was slow to catch on. Rachel and I still carpooled, she stopped speaking to me in the car. I was getting a severely cold shoulder that left me stranded and feeling very alone. I began noticing every eye roll, every insult and every private joke that kept me on the outs. Walking down the hall, I glued my eyes to the floor so I wouldn't accidentally make eye contact with anyone. I was afraid that if I did, they would make fun of me too. It was pretty clear that I was no longer a pea in anyone's pod.

I felt like a total social loser and all I could do was wish things were going to get better. *Guess* jeans were the fashion standard that year. Still desperate to fit in but unable to afford the expensive clothes worn by the popular girls, I remember buying a pair of *Jet* jeans. Please don't confuse these with the *Jet* jeans worn by celebrities these days. My *Jets* were decidedly off-brand, but I thought they were cool enough.

I was a timid *Jet* jeans girl in a *Guess* jeans world, and the older 8th grade girls noticed. More importantly, they noticed that I was always alone and that I was afraid to make eye contact. That made for some lonely months of being openly and relentlessly teased about my clothes. I hated school. I got stomachaches and wanted to stay home. One day on the bus back from sports, I sat alone in the front row behind the driver while the 8th grade girls pelted food at the back of my head. I remember thinking if I just stayed quiet and didn't look at them they would stop. They didn't. Why were these girls, and every girl at my school, so mean? I just didn't get it.

The sad irony is that my parents were shelling out tons of money they didn't have to give me a fantastic education in this private school, but all I could focus on was becoming invisible. I never engaged in class. I never raised my hand. I was so afraid of people seeing me, and not liking what they saw that I tried to disappear. Have you ever felt that way?

Somehow, someway, I survived the teasing, isolation, exclusion and bullying during middle school. Looking back, I can see that I spent my energy protecting myself and putting up walls so that people wouldn't see the real me. I always wondered what would happen if they saw or knew the real me. How would they treat me then?

Every one of us needs a safe place where we can just be real and be ourselves, especially in middle school. That's the reason I started "Michelle In the Middle." It's a place where we "middle-school survivors" can talk honestly about all things middle-school, from memories (both good and bad) to how to survive as parents of middle-schoolers. Just when I thought I was done with The Middle, I've got a sixth grader. Middle School is back in my life and this time I'm going in with my head up and the walls down.

For all you middle-school parents out there who could use some support, visit me at MichelleintheMiddle.com or on Facebook (www.facebook.com/middleschoolrelief).

SHINE

Social bullying is a very difficult type of bullying to address. The social hierarchy of elementary and middle-school girls can be complex. There are subtle (and sometimes not-so-subtle) cues and hints that designate how one should behave or not, who someone should speak with and who should be ignored. There are many unwritten rules involved and these rules have serious consequences. Often, girls are more conscious of and more concerned with interpersonal relationships than boys are. Relationships and social status become increasingly more important, and directly related to their self-esteem. It's all about *fitting in*, and often girls will do and say things that feel inauthentic and demoralizing just to affirm their social standing.

Our girls have so much going for them. When they are younger, they will sing out, dance like crazy, and wear silly costumes in public, all without one care about what they look like. They feel free to express themselves, and we are happy to see their freedom. Then something happens. They start school, and they get a little older. They start to see clubs and cliques form, they watch kids separate and divide, they hear name-calling and gossip for the first time, and possibly they join in. As they begin to judge others, it makes sense that they start to judge themselves. The self-esteem that was once off the charts has now shrunk to a dim light. By the way, I know boys have some of these experiences too.

What can we do about it? First, we can make sure that we teach our young girls that the most important thing is who they are as a person, and how they choose to treat people. When we teach girls to make choices based on what feels healthy and best, it becomes a habit that is stronger than the need to fit in.

Another thing we can do to support healthy self-esteem in our girls is to compliment and validate them on all of their achievements, especially the accomplishments they are most proud of themselves. Too much emphasis is placed on appearance. Their self-worth should not be determined by a pair of jeans.

Somewhere along the way, our girls have learned to hide themselves. Their skills and talents get buried, and when that happens we all lose out. Let's nurture their self-esteem and remind our girls and ourselves of the freedom they once had as little kids and support them to express their intelligence, their strengths, their feelings and all their gifts to everyone around them. When we take the time to celebrate the gifts that each has to offer, and we support them to shine brightly in their own unique way, they will learn that acknowledgement and validation feels much better than gossiping and bullying. When they feel good and respect themselves, they will also be able to appreciate healthy relationships with other girls.

CHALLENGE

What are some of the ways girls and women are mean to one another? What are the reasons you think this happens? Where did girls and women learn to be so hard on themselves and others? In this lesson we shared how way too much emphasis is put on appearance. Think of a girl or woman in your life that deserves an acknowledgement for her *achievements* and share it with her.

CHAPTER 13
RAFAEL

D on't be a wuss.
Stand up and be a man.
Be stronger.
Toughen up.

Growing up in my neighborhood was no joke. My older
brother and his buddies used to run the streets doing
drugs, tagging and making sure everyone knew they were
the baddest dudes around. That was their world, and they
wanted to make sure I grew up tough just like they were.
To help me out with that, they beat me up every day. Verbally, they teased me for wearing glasses and for being big.
Physically, they hit me so I could learn how to be strong
and take it like a man. For a nine-year-old boy, it was

hard to take. If that was what being a man was all about, I wasn't sure I was ready for it.

That went on for a few years until I started middle school, and the tables turned. I had toughened up just like my brother and his friends had wanted me to. Instead of being bullied, I was the bully. I learned to box, I got involved with sports at school, and by the time I was in high school, I was a jock and a "real man." I was popular and knew that when I said something people would listen. Too bad I used that power to hurt others. I used my words to cut people down, and no one was off-limits. I would see a weakness in someone and make a joke about it right to their face. I would put down their clothes, their looks, the way they walked, who they hung out with, and on and on. I could find something bad to say about everyone--I knew how to verbally hit them where it hurt. I got attention, and people laughed at my jokes, so at the time it made me feel like it wasn't so bad.

One day my buddies and I were clowning on some kid in our class. We were calling him a nerd and a suck up. This kid did the thing that most kids never do--he answered back. He responded to my comment with a smart-ass clever comment of his own. He stood up for himself and that made me shut my mouth! One of my buddies wouldn't let up, he kept going, and this kid had some great comebacks, so now my buddy looked like a fool. Well, he could tell this kid was making him look bad, so he stood up and punched him in the face. Whoa, that was definitely taking this too far! If you can't take what you dish out, you probably shouldn't be saying it.

It's a crazy cycle we're all in. One day telling someone not to bully and then turning around and doing it yourself. There seems to be no end to it. I know I've done some bad

stuff in my life--too many fights, too involved in violent activities, and I've said too many bad things to a lot of people.
If you really knew me, deep down I have a very kind heart.
I'm sure that may be hard for you to believe at this point,
but it's true.

I'm doing my best to turn things around, though sometimes
I still mess up. I got myself into counseling, and I'm working on being a better person in the world. I don't want to
pass on any violence or bullying to anyone, especially my
baby daughter. To me, that's what being a man is all about.

MAN/KIND

We live in a world where our gender, or our perceived gender, comes with a set of rules about how we are supposed
to behave. Though none of us asked for these rules, we
all live within them, even while we are working to change
them. In Rafael's story, we address how gender stereotyp-
ing impacts young men, especially in schools.

Every day boys and men are bombarded with messages
about what it means to be a man and to be a boy. They hear
messages like "be tough" or "be strong," and yet when they
go to school and act tough, they get in trouble for it. They
are given the message to "handle their business" which
often turns into some type of harmful and aggressive behavior. Our boys are trapped in a swirling world of mixed
messages.

Here's a snapshot of what's happening with our boys:
- Boys are more likely to be held back
- More boys are enrolled in special education classes
  than girls

- Boys are more likely to be labeled or diagnosed with a learning disability
- Boys are hit more often in homes
- Boys are four times more likely to be prescribed Ritalin. Currently over one million boys in the United States take Ritalin daily.
- Boys are less likely to go to college than girls
- Boys are slower to develop impulse control than girls
- 95% of all juvenile homicides are committed by boys

Rafael learned what it meant to be a man from his older brother and his friends. He learned that getting beat up every day toughens you. Boys get these messages, and we wonder why we have teasing, bullying and violence in our communities.

Some boys come to school with feelings they don't know how to deal with, and it shows up as wrestling, hitting, throwing things and fighting. We get tired of yelling at them to stop, and when they won't or can't, we punish them. This cycle continues day after day. Look at the above statistics again. What future is most likely for these boys?

If this wasn't bad enough, our language and attitude with them gets more severe, and we start to label them as troublemakers, bad kids or bullies. We exile them, bench them and even try to humiliate them into compliance. It never works. Their "bad" behavior can stop for a while, but the feelings remain. Maybe instead of looking at their behavior, we can take a moment to look at our own.

Are our traditional schools the best environments for our boys? Are they thriving, growing and being taught in ways that are in line with their development? As our schools focus more heavily on test scores, there is less time for play. Sitting our children in chairs for over 1,000 hours every year doesn't seem fair.

Let's find ways to meet the physical, emotional and academic needs of our boys. Let's model effective communication skills, positive play and engagement in activities that will foster their academic skills.

Like Rafael, boys are going to learn about what it means to be a man from the men in their lives. Surrounding them with a variety of positive role models will lay the foundation for them to grow into healthy and positive young men.

CHALLENGE

Who are the positive male role models in your life? Who has had the most impact or influence on you? Does this person know you appreciate him? Let him know three reasons you are glad he is in your life.

CHAPTER 14
MAX

Disruptive. Talking out in class. Odd gestures. Being "weird." Socially inappropriate.

That's my son. He's twelve years old, but emotionally, he's more like eight. He's in middle school where all the other kids are experimenting with their coolness and trying to find their groups and their identities. My son doesn't have the social or emotional awareness of his peers, so to them, he's odd, strange, weird.

What they don't know is that he has special needs--my sweet son has autism. As a baby, Max developed like any other child, but then after a couple of years, we started to see signs that something was different. He wasn't really talking or speaking much, so we took him in for testing. The results confirmed that Max was autistic--he was five years old.

Life changed after that. We had to learn about autism, and we had to figure out the best ways to support and care for him. After his diagnosis, we did everything we could to create an environment that would make life easier for him and for the entire family. Though that time was definitely a challenge, and I had feelings of sadness, frustration, confusion and anger, we were ready to do whatever it took to provide a happy and loving world for my son.

In elementary school Max was put in classes that gave him the structure and environment that supported him. The teachers taught to his needs, and he flourished. In fact, he did so well that he was able to integrate back into regular classrooms. That's a big deal! Our best efforts to make life "normal" for Max were working. And then he started middle school.

Instead of empathy, understanding and compassion, Max has faced rejection and degrading insults. They misunderstand his gestures and odd behaviors, which give other kids an excuse to put him down and call him names. The students don't know or understand him, and they aren't interested in learning about him. It's a big school with a thousand students, and Max's special needs are easily overlooked and usually ignored, even by the administrators. Though some of his teachers give him the space and support he needs, it's not enough.

Since every student in middle school is trying to figure out where they belong on the social ladder, no one is willing to extend a hand of friendship to Max. He's usually a target to make fun of--no one wants to be associated with the "freak." Max has impulses that are difficult for him to control, and when the administrators tell him to "act better" and he can't, he gets in trouble and is sent home. If my son could act better, he would. And while being bullied by other students is not right, being bullied by school administrators is inexcusable.

In class one day, a kind student offered Max a cracker. He popped the cracker in his mouth without realizing that it had tuna on it--Max is not a fan of tuna. Immediately he started spitting the cracker out of his mouth while making loud "ick" noises. Of course everyone around him stopped and stared because they had no idea what was happening. Max had no idea that he was being disruptive. He went to the principal's office for the incident where he was scolded and told to "knock it off." There was no consideration for Max and his autism. Both Max and I were furious.

Max has special needs, but don't we all? Who doesn't have a special ritual they do to calm down or feel comforted. Who doesn't have a special way they tie their shoes or eat their food or brush their teeth? What weird or strange thing do you do?

I don't want my son to be surrounded by bullying and have him be a target because of his special needs. I want my son to go to a school where students and adults are willing to learn, to understand, and to accept any student with all of their special needs. Most of all, I want my son to feel the respect that every human deserves.

EVERYONE BELONGS

I agree with Max's mom that every human deserves respect.

I also believe that every child deserves to go to a school that is safe, fun and bully-free.

In this story, Max's mom points out that we all have special needs. Some of us need special help with reading or math, some with our shyness, and others with our dance moves. Things that may be difficult for some come naturally and easily for others. Maybe we're designed this way so we can learn to discover each person's unique talent. Then once discovered, we can come together, each with our own skill to contribute in the best way possible.

Everyone wants to feel like they belong, to know that they have their place. Belonging helps us feel safe and is essential to our growth, especially in our younger years. As children this is easy--we look around, and everyone we see is a friendly face. We're not concerned about social status, the clothes people wear, or the color of their skin--we just see a friend, someone to play with. The sandbox is neutral ground where everyone belongs.

As we get older that neutral ground begins to fall away. What's on the outside becomes more important than what's on the inside. Some people or groups have all the outside things that give them power, while other people or groups are stripped of any power or status. This is oppression--unjust treatment of a person or group of people.

During the interview with Max's mom, I had a few short moments to speak with Max. I asked him how he wanted to be treated at school. He told me that he wants the other kids to stop calling him bad names and that he wants to be treated like any other kid.

CHALLENGE

Notice what groups or people have the power in your
school or community. Notice the people who have less
power or are oppressed. What status do you have? What
is one way you can help to create neutral ground or to even
out the playing field? It takes only one person to create a
shift.

CHAPTER 15
JACQUI

How would you feel if you showed up at school one day, and you had no friends? How would you feel if one day you had twenty friends, and the next day you had zero? Have you ever felt alone? Were you ever kicked out of a friendship?

My name is Jacqui, and when I was in the 8th grade everything was great. I had plenty of friends to talk to and to hang out with, and being a part of the group was normal and easy. I never had to think about being alone or wonder who I would spend time with. I was just a kid having fun at school surrounded by all of my friends.

At one point during that 8th grade year, I got really sick

and had to stay home for two weeks. I didn't like being away from school, and I missed my friends. After those two weeks of being at home and mostly alone, I was happy to get back to school and see all of my friends. Of course I expected things to pick up exactly where I had left them. I expected people to be excited to see me and to catch up on what had been happening at school. I expected things to be normal. But something changed--something was different. I don't know how it happened or even why it happened, but when I returned to school, I returned to no friends. The twenty friends I used to talk to and be with two weeks before--gone--including my best friend from kindergarten. How does this happen? Who decides to kick someone out of a friendship? What makes us do this to each other? There are no words to describe what it feels like.

How could I have done anything to hurt or offend someone while I was out sick? I tried to figure out what I did, and to this day I still don't know. I had become an outcast. When I tried to talk to former friends, they turned their backs and ignored me. I was excluded from hanging out, left out of social events, and pretty much erased from their lives. As time went on and I kept getting left out and ignored, my mother stepped in. She spoke to some of the girls' mothers and to staff at the school. After many conversations with other moms and promises from the teachers that they would keep an eye out for me, nothing really changed. The teachers had no idea how to make this better for me.

While nothing changed with the situation, something started to change inside me. I was stressed out all the time. In order to make myself feel better, I started to overeat and then binge. I was in the eighth grade, and I had an eating disorder. Everything was wrong and out of control, and bingeing was the only thing that helped me feel better, even for just a moment.

I lived with stress, name calling, teasing and being a total outcast at school for six months before we all moved on to the high school. I stayed away from my previous "friends" and started to make new ones. Thankfully, I found other girls who were not into gossiping or drama and weren't interested in excluding others. They were girls like me who just wanted to belong and have other friends who were nice and kind.

My eighth grade experience was traumatic and devastating, and it had a lasting impression on me. I learned a lot about friendship and the importance of being kind and accepting to others.

I'm older now and I'm a parent. When my son started going to school, I definitely didn't want him to experience anything like I did. One day I had a conversation with my son, and he shared with me how he was being bullied at school.

There was a kid who would find my son in isolated areas--in the hallway, in the bathroom, even in the lunch line and just pick on him and call him names.

This other boy had bullied my son for four years before I realized it. Wow! How did this happen without me knowing? I went to the principal, the superintendent, and the other boy's mother. It stopped for a little bit, but then it started back up. The school didn't have any concrete policy on how to handle bullying, so I was on a mission to make sure that my son did not experience what I went through. No way!

My son is a nice, kind, soft-spoken child. Many people say we should teach our kids to stand up for themselves. For some kids, that comes easy. For other kids like my son, it's more challenging. My son needed my help in voicing his feelings and opinions. He wasn't going to stand up to the other kid--it just isn't in his nature. How many other kids feel like my son? How many of them feel even worse about themselves when they don't or can't stand up for themselves? As adults, it's our responsibility to help our children navigate these tough waters. The mom of the other boy really tried to get her son to stop bullying. When it started up again, she was deeply embarrassed and ashamed that she couldn't control her son's behavior--she didn't have the skills to stand up to her own eight-year-old son.

When I realized that no one knew what to do or how to deal with our situation, I knew our school and our district needed help, the same help I could have used when I was in school. Instead of blaming the school and causing more conflict, I decided to take action. Along with another parent whose kid was being bullied, we created a resource guide for parents at our school. We wanted every parent to have guidelines and know clear steps of what to do if their child was being bullied. This resource has turned into a book that is now helping lots of families not just in our school, but throughout our entire state. I'm glad my experience turned into something that could help other schools, kids and families.

Jacqui is the co-author of *When Your Child Is Being Bullied: Real Solutions for Parents, Educators & Other Professionals.* Visit her website for information that can help your school be a safer place at www.solutionsforbullying.com.

BE THE CHANGE

Mahatma Gandhi once said, "Be the change you wish to see in the world."

There is no school that is untouched by the violence and pain of children hurting each other. Studies show that bullying in schools and bullying online continue to rise. Surveys reveal that nearly 77% of students have been the victim of one or more types of bullying. Who knows how much more bullying might be occurring that isn't getting reported. It is estimated that nearly 60% of children admit to *not* telling an adult when they are being bullied.

Schools are struggling with overcrowded classrooms, a shortage of counselors, and underfunded sports, music, and art programs, all of which adds to our youth's needs not getting met. Our young people are crying out for attention and desperately waiting for us to respond. As adults we can blame and complain about how the system is failing our students, or we can take a stand to make the most impact that we possibly can.

Jacqui's story is an example of a parent taking an action for good or "being the change." Instead of fueling the fire and continuing the cycle of bullying, she approached the problem with the right attitude. Instead of standing by, she did what needed to be done to ensure her son would be safe and that he could attend a school that had a clear policy on bullying. Her action supported her child and supported children in other families throughout her district and state.

Everyone has the power to make a difference. It takes each of us to make true change happen. There are many, many ways to help. We can educate children, teachers and parents. We can be counselors and mentors to children and their families. We can help our schools develop hands-on, empathetic approaches and policies that take people beyond punishing behavior to transforming schools into positive and caring climates.

Our hats are off to you, Jacqui, and the many other people out there who are *Being the Change,* who are digging deep and giving their best in an effort to help thousands upon thousands of children live in a safe, caring, fun and bully-free world.

CHALLENGE

What change would you like to see in regard to bullying in schools? How can you help your school or your community be a better place? What inspiration or support do you need to step into action and **Be the Change**? No more waiting, the time is now!

CHAPTER 16
DON

I grew up loving and adoring my parents--they were my world! My father worked hard and always looked after me, and my mother was devoted and affectionate. Although my mother loved me, she struggled with alcohol addiction that kept her from being there 100%. I also had an older brother who had a lot of anger towards me just because I was born. He used to punch me and beat on me every chance he got. He made my home a living hell.

In elementary school, I was endlessly teased and always sought the protection of my teachers. I was called a "sissy," a "wuss," "teacher's pet" and a bunch of other names I can't say here, but I'm sure you get the picture.

In middle school the teasing and bullying became aggressive with people threatening to beat me up after school and physically pushing and shoving me around. I got "bumped" into in the hallways more times per day than anyone else. I absolutely hated going to school--wouldn't you?

Then one day, amidst all of this torment, something unthinkably bad happened. My dad died. I was twelve years old, and this was the person who I drew my strength from. I tried to reach out to my mother, but she was trying to heal herself. I didn't want to add to her troubles, so I did what a lot of people do--I kept it all inside. I was about to start high school, and I knew the harassment, teasing, and bullying would continue and probably would get even worse. I couldn't bear it, so I decided to stop going to school.

I made up notes, faked my report card and wandered the streets. There was no way I was going to spend all day in a building where I was disrespected, pushed around, and taunted. I knew any day I could be forced to go back to school and as a precautionary measure of that happening, I wrapped a razor blade in cardboard and aluminum foil and carried it around in my pocket. I was prepared to die rather than endure the torture of being bullied at school another day.

I started hanging out at an ice skating rink just to find a safe place. I met a skating instructor who encouraged me to get on the ice. He was a skating coach who took me under his wing, and I was grateful. He was a smart, strong, male role model, which was exactly what I needed at the time. He coached me, and I became a good enough skater to enter competitions. I eventually became a national champion!

The coach and I became close, and eventually too close.

I felt things starting to get uncomfortable and just plain creepy. He was the only person in my life that cared, the only person who was helping me, and he knew it. One day, he crossed the line and forced me to do things that I didn't want to do. The man who was my only hope for safety and security was sexually abusing me. I was crushed.

It never seemed an option to tell anyone what was going on--I felt that I was on my own. I had survived so much already, and somewhere deep within I knew I could make it through this. I knew that first I had to get far away from this sick man who would continue molesting and abusing me. Luckily for me, I met a new coach who was safe and trustworthy, as well as an incredible teacher. There is nothing that I can say that could convey how much this man helped me, and the difference it made to have a positive and caring adult actually *believe in me*!

Looking back, I wish so many things could have been different for me. I wish school could have been a safe place. I wish an adult had intervened when I was being bullied. I wish the other kids could have accepted me as I was. I wish I had been a kid who easily fit in. I wish I had the support of other strong adults in my life to guide me along the way.

I started to see a counselor to help me heal some of my wounds. I went from being bullied at home by my brother, to losing my father, to being harassed at school and then to being abused. I had lived a lot of life before I was even twenty, and I was definitely in need of and absolutely ready for healthy support. Whatever you are going through, you can get through it. Reach out--there are people who want to support you. You are not alone. I believe in you.

SOMEWHERE TO BE

How could one person go through so much without anyone noticing? Reading this story, it seems unthinkable that
everyone could neglect this young man. Yet, I am sure there
are countless cases of nameless and faceless children, silent-
ly going through who-knows-what, without anyone to pay
attention to them, or any place to go where they are safe to
just be. Like Don, thousands of kids come to school each
day, feeling scared and unsafe. In one year in the United
States, 1.6 million to 2.8 million youth run away from home.
How many of them left home because they were in a situation like Don's?

Our classrooms and our homes are busy with the demands
of daily living in this modern world. Don's story is a prime
example of what happens when we don't pay close enough
attention to the lives of those around us. Look how far back
his problem started--it began in elementary school and fol-
lowed him into middle school. It kept growing and fester-
ing, compounded by the death of his father, until finally
in high school, he started carrying a razor blade to school,
both out of fear for his life and out of outrage for years of
torment!

This all could easily have been avoided if someone was listening and paying attention, and if someone took the time
to care for this boy. No one did, and it left him very vulnerable to one of the worst dangers of all--a sexual predator.

Have you ever wondered what was going on in the home
lives of the children that walk into your classroom every
day? Violence prevention research illustrates how emotional problems often show up as physical complaints, especially in children. Schools with high levels of aggression often

have significantly higher levels of visits to the nurse's office, as well as higher levels of tardiness and truancy. Is it any wonder? As Don shared, wouldn't you hate going to school if you were being treated poorly, especially if nobody even noticed or helped you?

We can and do have a powerful effect on each other. Check in with yourself to find ways you can make your home, school or classroom an even safer place for all kids.

Learn more about Don at www.enlightenmentofevil.com.

CHALLENGE

What makes you feel most safe? What does a safe school or home look, sound and feel like? Take a moment a write or draw what it would feel like, what it would look like and how people would treat one another. Share your thoughts with one other person and find one way you can step toward that ideal home or school.

CHAPTER 17
RACHEL

Quacker. Duck Face. Quack, quack, quack.

Imagine hearing that behind your back every time you walked down the hallway.

Imagine hearing people call you names but never say your real name.

Imagine hearing quacking and giggling whenever you walked into a room.

Imagine my life was your life. How would you feel?

What they didn't know was that my dad had just died. Because he died, I was forced to move in with my mom. I was the new kid at a new school, my dad was dead, I was being called quack face, and I didn't feel I could say or do anything without being judged or ridiculed. Talk about being kicked when you're already down--I can't even describe the pain of it to you.

I had been teased my entire life, so in some ways this wasn't new for me, but on top of my grieving and sadness, it was too much. Would they have called me those names if they really knew me?

The teasing and bullying wouldn't end, so I returned to my previous school, the one I went to when I lived with my dad. The bullying began there. First it was just two girls who kept pointing out that I had no friends. Soon enough someone who I thought was a friend joined in too. They called me names and when I would walk down the hall, they would throw things at me. It was bad enough having to endure that all day at school, but just when I thought it couldn't get any worse, the name-calling started online. Ugly. Fat. Worthless. When I responded to their comments online, it only made it worse. I thought I could battle them with words on a screen, but they found even more ways to tell me what a loser I was and how they were going to find me at school and physically hurt me.

The threats online got to a point where I felt I had to tell my mom. She had no idea how I was being treated at school, and she had no clue that the put-downs and name-calling were now happening online for everyone to see. She talked to the school, and because of the physical threats, the school had to bring in the police. The families of the other students involved were talked to by the police, and thankfully it all stopped.

I know how bullying hurts. I watch the news and see how

other kids are committing suicide because they just want to escape the painful teasing, taunting and name-calling.

On my 16th birthday, I decided to give myself the gift of making a difference, of doing something with my life that actually mattered. I wasn't going to stand by and just do nothing anymore! So for my birthday, I started my own Facebook page called "Stand Up, Speak Out" to help put an end to bullying forever! I want to get the message out that hurting or harming yourself in any way is not an answer to your problems, though it may feel like it at the time.

On my site, www.standupspeakout-endbullying.com I have a page called "The Creative Corner" that is all about healthy positive self-expression. Instead of hurting yourself or others, express yourself creatively and email your work to me. I want to know how you feel and help you have a voice about your experiences. The cool thing is that by sharing your hurt and pain, you can make a difference for someone else.

REAL CONNECTION

Being bullied in any form causes stress and impacts the way we see ourselves and the way we see the world. Rachel was verbally and emotionally bullied as well as bullied online.

Here's what we should know about online bullying:
- 43% of kids have been bullied while online. 1 in 4 have had it happen more than once.
- 35% of kids have been threatened online. Nearly 1 in 5 have had it happen more than once.
- 53% of kids admit having said something mean or

hurtful to another person online. More than 1 in 3
have done it more than once.

* 58% have not told their parents or an adult about
something mean or hurtful that happened to them
online.

With technology moving so fast, it's a challenge for us to
keep up with it all.

Here are some helpful tips for internet safety that can prevent cyber-bullying:

1. Unplug: Set hours when all technology is turned off
    and put away. Both adults and young people need
    to take time for actual face time--that's not Facebook
    time! This will monitor online activity for everyone
    and put some limits to its use at home and in the
    classroom.
2. Connect: Instead of connecting to a device, spend
    time connecting with and to another human. The
    reason so many young people do not say something
    when they are bullied online is because they may
    not feel like they have someone to talk to. Check in
    with your students or kids about how they are being
    treated online.
3. Monitor: 7.5 million Facebook users are under
    thirteen and 5 million are under eleven years old.
    According to Facebook, you must be at least thirteen
    years old to open an account. Monitor all digital de-
    vices and online activity with respect to your young
    person or student.

Rachel didn't let cyber-bullying stop her from creating
something online that could help other youth. Her efforts are a great example of the good that could come out
of online communities. If your students or young people

love social media, support them to get involved with online communities that are positive or to interact with sites that support their passions.

CHALLENGE

Instead of spreading negative comments over the internet, think about using social media to acknowledge or appreciate someone. Who has done something for you lately? Appreciate their friendship or kind act through your social media networks. Spread a positive rumor that will make someone's day!

CHAPTER 18
CHERYL

I was a disaster. I was a target in the making for bullies. I was a scared little girl and a loner. My parents were both out working all the time, and I was left to navigate the world on my own. I was easy prey for anyone.

As I grew up, I knew I lived in a bully-or-be-bullied world. In elementary school, I got beat up and didn't even know what it meant to stand up for myself.

Then 6th grade happened. There were these two girls, Jodie and Chandra, and they were tough and mean. One day they approached me on the playground. I'm not sure how it happened, but I was ready to stand up for myself. When I looked at them I was pretty sure this situation was going to end badly for someone--probably me! They got in my face, asking if I wanted to fight them. I just stood up to them, got back in their face, and looked them in the eyes. It was clear I wasn't backing down. On the outside it probably looked like I wasn't scared, but on the inside I was freaking out!

Because of my reaction, they accepted me, and I joined their little gang that went around terrorizing everybody. We caused all kinds of trouble, and by the end of 6th grade, I got kicked out of school for forcing another student to skip school and hang out. She told her parents I kidnapped her, so that was the end of the 6th grade for me.

Here's the truth--I was scared. In fact, I was terrified. I was doing all these things, but on the inside I was a lonely little girl with a big gaping hole on the inside. Bullying gave me a false sense of power. If I had real power, why would I feel the need to take yours? In the moment, the bullying felt good, but in the next moment I felt like a jerk and was left with all this shame about what I had done.

When I watched other kids playing, laughing, and being kids, all I really wanted was to go out and play too. I didn't know how to do that. The more trouble I got into, the more separated and removed I became, like being in the picture, but not in the frame.

By middle school, I started drinking and using drugs. The same thing happened. I would feel good in the moment, but then the shame would creep in, and it was unbearable. In order not to deal with my feelings, my emptiness or my loneliness, I kept on drinking and using drugs--for the next seventeen years!

After finding myself with no home, no job and no money,

I knew it was time to get sober--I needed serious help. It took some time, but eventually I learned to talk about my problems and to put words to that emptiness in my heart. I knew I had hurt other people and myself because I didn't know what else to do with what I felt on the inside. My sister was also in recovery, and her help was invaluable. For the first time I allowed someone to help me in a positive way, and I learned to stop pushing people away. I've been sober for fifteen years now. I am so proud of myself!

BE THERE

Cheryl's parents struggled with their relationship to each other. Both had high-powered jobs that kept them busy and away from home and from their kids. Cheryl was left alone a lot, and she did what she needed to do to survive without the ongoing consistent supervision of adults.

One question I asked while doing these interviews was, "What do you wish the adults in your life would have done differently?" Regardless of how loving, caring and supportive some of the parents and teachers were, most of them did not know what was happening to their child or student and didn't have the skills to effectively manage the situation.

Here are some things our interviewees wished the adults could have said to them:
"I'm sorry the kids are treating you so badly at school. What do you need?"
"I'm here. Tell me all about it."
"I love you, and I'm sorry they can't see all the great things that I see in you."
"You're not alone, and we'll take care of this together."

Our kids need us not just to be around, but also to be engaged, which means having conversations, and learning about what they are experiencing and feeling at home and at school.

In addition, the interviewees wished they could have had these things from the adults in their lives:
- Hugs and affection.
- Reassurance.
- A clear action plan to stop the bullying, such as going to the principal, talking to teachers, or talking to other parents.
- Compassion instead of blame for the bullying.
- Solving the problem appropriately. Outrage and drama from parents only makes it worse.

No matter the age, children need their parental figures and adults in their lives. They want the support, comfort and encouragement from a healthy, positive role model, even if it seems like they don't. At first, really connecting can feel awkward and strange. Maybe there isn't anything to say or you don't know what to say--that's okay. Stay with the connection, and the words will come. Everyone wants to be seen and heard--both youth and adults. Imagine what our relationships would be like if we took the effort each day to connect--even five minutes of getting real with someone--and we allowed someone to do the same with us. Wouldn't we all have the support we needed? Wouldn't we feel more comfortable telling the people around us the truth about what's happening? Wouldn't we be more likely to share our hurts, fears and pains with one another? If kids had that kind of support at school and home, would there be a need for bullying?

CHALLENGE:

Who has been an adult who has supported you in your life? What did he or she do that encouraged you? Call or text that person and let that special person know the impact he or she has had on you. Mentors, role models, teachers, guardians and parents often go overlooked. Take a moment and appreciate them.

CHAPTER 19
ALDO

FAG! FAGGOT! Is there a put down that is worse than that one? How would you feel if that's what your own father called you? Every. Single. Day. He actually called me "mariconcito," which is Spanish for "little faggot," Nice one, Dad.

I grew up in Koreatown in downtown Los Angeles. But I wasn't Korean--I was Latino, even if I didn't look like it. At first, kids thought I was white with my blonde hair and fair skin. Once I opened my mouth and they heard my accent, "wetback" was what I heard. Kids teased me for being Latino and called me names at school, and my family put me down at home. That's a bit harsh for a little kindergartener, don't you think?

I was feminine and girlie, and my father hated me for being that way. Instead of watching sports with my dad and
brothers, I would sit and cry over telenovelas (Spanish soap
operas) with my mom and sister. I preferred Barbie and My
Little Pony to Tonka Trucks and G.I. Joe. Every time my
mother gave me the toys I wanted, my father would go into
a rage, screaming at her to buy me "little man toys" instead
and admonishing her for encouraging me to be "that way."
It was pretty much a family brawl.

Our family was under constant financial stress, and my
mom sometimes took on two or three jobs. When she was
at work, I was left alone to deal with my dad and paternal-
grandmother's constant insults. Once he got going, he
would encourage my older brothers to join in. I guess he
thought if they called me a sissy or a fag enough times, I
would just change. Well, that didn't happen.

We all felt the stress of being in our home. My mom was
always working, my parents were constantly fighting, my
siblings got in trouble, and I got picked on. My escape was
locking myself in the bathroom, running the water and
staying in the tub for as long as I could. I would hear my
father's critical voice in my head while I tried to figure out
what was wrong with me--why didn't I like "little man
toys?" Why wasn't I like my brothers? I didn't have any
answers, just confusion. Sitting in that tub, I would cry and
try to drown myself. Believe me, it's not that easy to do,
and I know because almost every day of elementary school
I tried. Until I was ten years old, I was sad, angry and
lonely, and I just wanted to die.

I knew from an early age that I was gay. Yes, the dolls,
the clothes and the telenovelas were all clues. I started
to feel how different I was from my brothers. I started to
have crushes on boys, and in my family that wasn't just

wrong--it was a sin. In middle school I tried to "man up" by becoming the bully at school and picking on kids the way I was bullied at home. I would especially tease the kids who had accents or who were girlie boys or tomboy girls--basically, anyone who reminded me of me. I guess I figured if I threw the attention on them, no one would point those things out about me. How could I admit I was gay? I had been shamed by my father my entire life, and I saw how the kids at school used the word "gay" as a put down. I just didn't want to accept it, but I couldn't run away from myself forever. At least for the time being, I knew I was willing to fight to stay alive.

Thankfully, my friends in high school helped me see that bullying others was not the answer to dealing with my hurt feelings. That's when it dawned on me that I needed to start learning to love myself so that I could heal. I realized that the "Golden Rule" doesn't only apply to others--it begins within you.

By the time I went away to college, I felt I finally had room to breathe and just be myself. I experienced a freedom I never had before and it was amazing! At nineteen, I was ready to come out as a gay man to my family. I loved my family, and I didn't want to live a lie with them anymore. I didn't want to be one of those families that gets together, puts on fake smiles and pretends everything is just fine when we know it's not. I wanted a real relationship with them, and I was willing to take this risk. I was scared about this and thought about how they might react--would they disown me, yell at me, tell me I was going to hell or look at me with disgust?

The first person I told in the family was my mom. She was absolutely supportive and also concerned about me telling the rest of my family. At this point my dad was out of our lives. My parents had divorced and he moved back to Guatemala. I hardly ever heard from him, but my brothers were still around--the ones who often joined my dad in calling me "little faggot." I wanted to come out to them, and I had my reasons for being nervous about that.

Six months after coming out to my mom, we had a holiday family gathering and I felt this was the time to come out to everyone. So after a lifetime of being scared to be myself, and after months of agonizing and worrying about this moment, here it was. In front of my entire family--my sister, my brothers, their wives and my Mom--I said the truth. I'm gay.

In that next moment all I felt was their love. Their arms were around me and tears were in our eyes. Whew! No one was one bit surprised. They were incredibly accepting and very happy for me. One brother and his wife were really glad because they thought their son was going to be gay when he grew up, and they actually wanted me to be a positive role model for him. I didn't have to hide anymore. I could just be myself with the people I love the most. What a relief!

I was bullied for being gay. I was bullied for being Latino. I was bullied for the clothes I wore. I had lived so much of my life being oppressed and feeling like I just couldn't be the real me. I allowed my hurt feelings to become my excuse for becoming a bully myself --to torment others and add to their grief, instead of helping them. I was fortunate to have made friends with good people who were brave enough to point out the error of my ways and who pushed me to be a better me. It was that self-love that I needed in order to take the risk of finally telling my family.

It's ok to just come out and be honest, and to let people

know who you are. If you are reading this and are going through something similar, I hope you will do whatever it takes for you to have your freedom to be yourself and to stop hurting yourself or others. I finally found my freedom, and let me tell you, there is NOTHING like it!

FREE TO BE

Putting people down is popular nowadays. We pick at others and point out their faults. Every detail of our uniqueness becomes a target of other people's disapproval and judgment. We push each other away because we have different eye color, a different faith, or because we live on the other side of town. We put people down because they are a different racial and ethnic group or because they have different sexual preferences. All this path ever creates is more loss, more isolation, more confusion, more self-loathing and more destructive behaviors.

Probably no group knows these things more than the Lesbian/Gay/Bisexual/Transgender (LGBT) population. Studies show that nearly 9 out of every 10 LGBT students have been bullied within the past year. Estimates further show that nearly 30% of all completed suicides are related to sexual identity crises. LGBT students are also *five times more likely* to miss school due to feeling unsafe as a result of prior sexual identity bullying they had endured, with 28% of LGBT students dropping out of school entirely. This isn't just a little problem, this is an epidemic that ruins, and often takes the lives of, young people.

One of the best things we can do for others, if not *the* best thing, is to accept and appreciate them *exactly as they are*. When we lay down our preferences, assumptions and opinions about how we believe people should be, and begin to appreciate them for who they are, their worth arises, like warmth filling the air at dawn. Something else begins to happen that is equally as amazing: We begin to love *ourselves* in that same way--*just as we are*.

What would our schools be like if we were able to dismiss our judgments and opinions for a while, and allow ourselves to accept each other as we truly are? Can you imagine being able to tell people *exactly* who and what you love, how you feel, what you need, and having that actually *celebrated*? What if you shared your most beautiful aspirations with someone and heard in response, *"That is awesome! How can I best support you?"*

As Aldo states in his story, there is nothing like freedom. Let's give each other that gift of acceptance so every one of us can truly be *Free to BE!*

CHALLENGE

In Aldo's story he tells us that it's okay to come out and be honest. What is something you can be honest about? All of us hide things about ourselves for fear of being ridiculed, laughed at, put down or bullied and when that happens we are not free. What's one thing you can share with someone about yourself that you've been hiding? Find the courage to share it someone who is trustworthy and give yourself a little more freedom today.

RESOURCES

Stop Bullying Now: http://www.stopbullying.gov/
The U.S. Department of Health and Human Services has
a comprehensive website with resources for both students
and adults.

Stop Bullying Speak Up: www.stopbullyingspeakup.com
The Cartoon Network has on-line resources for students
and parents.

The Anti-Defamation League: adl.org/combatbullying
The ADL offers workshops, training, curriculum and other
resources for schools.

GLSEN (The Gay, Lesbian and Straight Education Network): www.glsen.org/bullying
Provides anti-bullying resources and works with educators, policy makers, community leaders and students on
the urgent need to address anti-LGBT behavior and bias in
schools.

The Trevor Project: www.thetrevorproject.org
24-hour national help line for gay and questioning teens
866 4U TREVOR

The National Center for Bullying Prevention:
www.pacer.org/bullying

**PACER (Parent Advocacy Coalition for Educational
Rights)** is a child advocacy group focused on students with
disabilities. They promote awareness and teach effective
ways to respond to bullying.

Common Sense Media: www.commonsensemedia.org/
Offers tips for navigating the internet safely and educates parents on monitoring their students' internet and media use.

Collaborative for Academic, Social and Emotional Learning: http://casel.org/
CASEL offers resources in building students' social and emotional skills.

Challenge Day: www.challengeday.org
Offers a powerful, one-day program for middle- and high-schools that focuses on respect and oppression.

No Bully: www.nobully.com
Offers support to schools and training for adults on how to run effective "Solution Teams."

SOUL SHOPPE INFO

Since 2001, Soul Shoppe has been providing character education, life-skills training and bullying prevention programs to schools.

Here are some quotes from students and staff regarding Soul Shoppe programs:

"Thank your for teaching me how important I am. Now I can believe in myself. Now maybe I can actually make a difference in life or in the world." *-4ᵗʰ grader*

"I would say that the time our school spent with Soul Shoppe was life-changing. I could see a light go on in the faces of students and teachers." *-H. Harding, Teacher, Spokane, WA* "Great! Best Bullying Assembly we have seen. The students were captivated during the entire presentation and are still using the language to this day! Look forward to the follow up." *-J. Reinfelder, Principal, Flushing, MI*

"Thank you for teaching us just how special and unique each of us are." *-5ᵗʰ grader*

It would be an honor for us to serve your school community. Here are some ways we can help:

Elementary School Assemblies
> *Free to Be:* This assembly gets to the heart of bullying. Using multi-media and student interaction, we'll learn about the three types of bullying and learn the reasons why we believe there is "no such thing as a bully."

> *Tools of the Heart:* This assembly teaches two essential tools to support students to get what they really want.

Students role-play and practice the tools during
the assembly.

B.F.F. (Beautiful Friends Forever): Teaches students
how to make friends and how being a real friend is an
important skill that also prevents teasing, put-downs
and bullying.

Peacemaker Program
We train 30-35 of your students to resolve conflicts using our
specially designed "Peace Path." Students step on the path
and "walk towards peace." Each step guides the students to
communicate their feelings and needs so the conflict can be
resolved peacefully.

In additional to these programs for students, we offer staff
in-services and parent programs. For more details about
these programs and all our offerings, visit our website:
www.soulshoppe.com